How to Care for Your Finch

CONTENTS

*We would like to thank the
following for permission to
photograph their stock:*
Hansards Pet Centre, Romsey,
Roger & Anita Horwood,
Emsworth,
Kevin Curtis

Photos by:
Frank Naylor,
Colin Jeal

KINGDOM

©2002 by Kingdom Books PO9 5TT ENGLAND
Printed in China through Printworks int. Ltd.

INTRODUCTION

The Finches are ideal birds for the home: they are small, quiet and colourful, and bring a hint of the tropical and the exotic into our lives. Most finches can be housed in the ordinary all-wire cages available at pet shops. The larger the cage the better, however, and the most practical type is the breeding or large stock cage, which is rectangular in shape. Many of the smaller species of finch do best in a box cage, which is a solid box with only one side wired.

All cages must allow for easy cleaning, watering and feeding, as well as the installation of perches. Perches are best made from natural tree branches of varying thicknesses and should not be placed over food or water receptacles. Natural perches are readily available, can be replaced easily when dirty, and are excellent for keeping the bird's feet healthy.

Outdoor aviaries are the ideal method of housing most finch species, and are necessary to obtain good breeding results from many of them, especially the more insectivorous forms such as waxbills. Do not, however, let this fact deter you from obtaining and keeping an interesting collection of finches in indoor cages.

A group of various finches in an indoor aviary.

Feeding

All the finches discussed in this book feed quite easily on a diet of seeds, greens and insectivore mixture. Different birds may prefer different seeds, but they should all be offered a wide selection. Prepared seed mixtures can be purchased from any good pet shop.

Finches can be divided into two categories for feeding purposes. The Finch mix or British finch mix is designed to cater for the 'true' finches of the family fringillidae. This mix contains a high percentage of oil-based seeds, which are also higher in protein than cereal seeds. Hemp is an oil-based seed which can be added to the mixture. It is best given to birds housed outside during the winter as it is a very concentrated source of energy, and your birds will become obese if they eat too much of it. Niger and blue maw are also oil-based seeds that can be added to the mixture.

Foreign finch mixtures are made mainly from cereal seeds such as millet and canary seeds. These mixtures form the basis of the diet for munias and waxbills. Cereal seeds contain high levels of carbohydrate. The two main types are millet and canary seed. There are several different varieties of millet, the most popular being Panicum.

Panicum millet is very light and is best fed in spray form to prevent the seeds being scattered too easily.

A pied Zebra Finch hen.

There are many other types of seed you can offer your finches, but the more unusual ones, such as teazle and lettuce, can be obtained only from seed merchants. However, they can be purchased from your pet shop in the form of 'tonic' or 'condition' foods. Although your birds will enjoy the addition of these foods at any time of the year, they are normally used to bring the birds into breeding condition, or to help through the moult.

Finches also appreciate soaked seeds. Using the finch mix that you normally feed to your birds, soak a small amount in warm water for 24 hours. Throw out the water and rinse the seed well before feeding it to your birds. Soaked seeds spoil easily and must be removed after a day. Only ever feed freshly soaked seeds. If kept moist and somewhere warm, such as an airing cupboard, soaked seeds will sprout. Finches love sprouted seeds which, again, should be washed thoroughly in case mould spores have developed. Some finches take other forms of fresh foods such as grated carrot or sweet apple. Experiment and find out what your bird likes.

You will need to provide livefoods if you want to breed your birds. Very few finch species are able to rear their young without a constant supply of insects. You can buy livefoods in packs from your local pet shop or you can breed your own. The most commonly-used foods are whiteworm, mealworms, crickets and fruit flies. It is also possible to collect creatures such as spiders and aphids from your garden, but make sure no pesticides are used in the area.

Finches kept in outside aviaries will be able to obtain a large percentage of livefood for themselves, but this may have to be supplemented when the young are in the nest.

As seed eaters, finches need to be able to grind down the seeds. This takes place in the gizzard with the help of grit. Therefore grit must always be available and is an excellent source of minerals.

A variety of greens should also be offered. Among the best are leaf lettuce, chickweed, spinach, dandelion and carrot tops, to name a few.

Other foods that may be given from time to time include boiled (at least 25 minutes) crumbled egg yolk, soaked ant eggs, milk-soaked whole wheat bread (not too sloppy), and insectivore or 'mynah bird' food.

A much appreciated treat can be provided by placing a clump of sod in any cage or aviary that lacks a natural earth floor. The birds find a lot of valuable food in the form of insects and tender grass shoots, and also benefit from eating some of the dirt.

Right: This is a white-breasted yellow Gouldian (cock) Finch. Generally, the male is more brightly coloured than the female.

HEALTH

Birds that are properly housed, fed and otherwise looked after seldom become ill. There are times, however, when disease or other ailments occur even in the best managed collections. The greatest drawback to treating sick birds (especially these small birds) is the fact that often their troubles do not show themselves until it is too late to do anything. Keep a sharp lookout for signs of trouble, which are sometimes difficult to detect. However, if you see a bird sitting with its feathers ruffled, with its head under its wing and both feet on the perch, something is likely to be wrong.

The most important and useful treatment for many (in fact most) bird ailments is heat. Remove any ailing bird to a hospital cage, which is fully enclosed with glass on the front and has means of maintaining a constant temperature in the region of 29-32°C (85-90°F). This cage should also have food bowls, a water bottle and you must be able to clean it.

When in use, this cage should be kept at a temperature of at least 29°C for about the first 24 hours, after which the heat can be lowered very gradually during each succeeding 24-hour period. This heat treatment often works wonders, and it is especially useful in cases of chills and egg-binding, and for many more obscure ailments.

Antibiotics are also of great value in treating many illnesses common to finches. It is important to get a sick bird to a veterinary surgeon as soon as possible so any medication prescribed has as much time as possible to work.

You should quarantine any birds new to your collection and keep them apart from the others for a period of at least two weeks. They should also be treated with a parasite-killing spray or powder to eliminate any lice or mites they may be carrying.

When you get your new finch home, place the carrying box inside the cage or aviary and let the bird find its own way out. Remember, it will take a few days for the bird to settle down, so avoid lots of noise or sudden movements near the cage or aviary.

Trimming The Nails

Occasionally you may have to trim the toe nails of some of these birds, especially those of certain nuns or mannikins. This simple operation can be performed with a pair of regular nail clippers or small scissors. The quick (the vein that runs into the claw) can be seen by holding the nail up to strong light. Do not cut into this, or the claw will bleed.

TRUE FINCHES

Some of the birds found in the family of true finches, Fringillidae, are among the most popular of all cage and aviary birds. This is the family to which the common canary belongs which, like the birds discussed below, is primarily a seed eater. Most of the finches also feed on insects, fruit and vegetable matter to varying degrees. All require grit for digestive purposes and must have a constant supply of water for drinking and bathing. Finches should also have some form of lime-containing material, such as cuttlebone or baked and finely ground egg shell, available to them at all times to help them produce good, hard-shelled eggs.

Males and females in many species differ in appearance, but some are very similar and can be sexed only by the behaviour or the song of the male. With few exceptions, finches build open, cup-shaped nests, and usually the female does all the nest building and incubation, which lasts 12 to 14 days. Both parents regurgitate food which the chicks take from their crops. The young finches leave the nest after about 14 or 15 days.

Most finches are quite hardy in respect to temperature but some, such as the Rainbow Bunting, cannot tolerate too much cold.

Most finches do not bother other birds except during the breeding season, although the larger species cannot be trusted with smaller birds.

Rainbow Bunting

The Orange-Breasted or Rainbow Bunting (*Passerina leclancheri*) comes from western Mexico and is one of the most beautiful of all finches. The male is turquoise blue on the back and wings, with apple-green on the crown of the head; his breast is orange, shading to yellow on the belly and underparts. The female is not so brightly coloured but mainly olive green with a trace of blue above and yellow below. Length, about 12.5cm (5in).

A selection of Finches in an indoor aviary.

This colourful little finch is not easy to breed in captivity. It should be given a wide variety of livefoods, especially if you want it to breed. Its diet should contain canary, millet, and wild grass seeds together with plenty of insectivore mixture.

Rainbow Buntings are somewhat delicate when first brought into more temperate climates and require controlled temperatures, but they soon become quite hardy.

Cuban Finch

Perhaps the best known of the small West Indian finches known as 'grass-quits' is the Cuban Finch (*Tiaris canora*). The male is yellowish green above; a black mask covers the face and is encircled by a broad yellow collar; the breast is black, shading into grey on the sides and abdomen. The female resembles the male but the black on the face is replaced with chestnut, and the yellow collar is smaller and duller in colour. Length, about 6.25cm (2.5in).

Unlike others of its family, this bird builds a spherical covered nest and often makes use of a nest box in captivity. The eggs are white, sometimes spotted with reddish-brown, and both sexes incubate. Young birds should be separated from their parents as soon as they are able to fend for themselves, or they are likely to be attacked and killed. Males are very pugnacious at all times towards others of their kind but are quite safe in mixed collections.

The diet for this species can contain canary, millet, and wild grass seeds along with insectivore mixture, greens, and so on.

European Goldfinch

The European Goldfinch (*Carduelis carduelis*) is a popular and well-known cage and aviary bird. It is often used for crossing with canary hens to obtain the singing 'mules' popular in Europe. The European goldfinch is native to Britain and therefore you can only buy captive bred birds.

In the male, the face is red, with a thin black line around the eyes and bill. The crown and a band descending down each side of the head and neck are white. Back, breast, and flanks are cinnamon-brown. The wings are black, with a broad transverse band of yellow, and white feather tips. The tail is black, with the inner webs tipped white. Belly, underparts, under and upper tail coverts are white. The bill is whitish. The female is very similar but duller in colour. The length is about 13.75cm (5.5in).

This species builds an open, cup-shaped nest of grass and roots mixed with down and, in captivity, readily nests in an open box or other cup-like receptacle. A clutch consists of four or five pale blue eggs which are speckled with brown. The hen alone incubates, and typically two broods are reared per season.

Food for this species may consist of a variety of seeds, including canary, millets, rape and niger, along with fruit, lettuce or other greens, mealworms, insectivore mixture, and so on. For a small bird, this species is very long-lived - individuals having been known to live as long as 27 years.

A White Breasted, Red Headed Gouldian Finch.

SPECIAL FINCHES

The most colourful and interesting of all small seed-eating cage birds are found in the family Estrildidae, which includes 107 true species inhabiting Africa, Asia, and Australasia. They are closely related to the true finches but differ in nesting habits; most of them build globular nests with side entrances that are entered by means of a spout. Additionally some have a 'cock's nest' added to the top of the structure in which the male sleeps alone. In captivity many of them accept partly-open boxes or other receptacles in which to construct their nests. Some are quite easily bred.

The eggs are white in colour, and incubation lasts for a period of 11 to 14 days. The males often share in this task. The nestlings show luminous and brightly-coloured swollen bands or spots at the gape, and dark spots or lines on the palate or the tongue or both, which are believed to be an aid to feeding in the darkness of the nest interior. Live insect food is needed for rearing the young of many species. Young birds leave the nest after about 18 to 21 days and are usually independent when about one month old. At first the plumage appears different from that of either parent but it matures by the end of the first year.

Most of these little birds are quite hardy, but they should be supplied with plenty of heat when first imported and preferably never kept in temperatures below 10-12°C (50-55°F). They can withstand lower temperatures, but do better if they are kept warm.

The majority are peaceful and get along well in mixed groups, although individuals vary and you must watch your collection for signs of fights and bullying.

None of these birds should be overcrowded in small quarters as they are prone to feather plucking and will soon become bald. Their diet consists of canary, millet, and wild grass seeds along with insectivore mixture, live insects, green food and fruit. Cuttlebone, grit and water for drinking and bathing are also necessary.

The smallest members of the family are known as 'waxbills' from the red sealing-wax appearance of their bills. They are found mainly in Africa, although two species come from Asia and one is native to Australia. They travel in large flocks which often contain several species, and their spherical nests are built in colonies. The cock performs a nuptial dance during which it holds a blade of grass in its bill which it offers to the hen.

Fledgling Finches in a wooden nest box.

Very few of the waxbills are what could be called easy to breed but some do so quite readily if properly cared for. They feed their young on insect food and success in breeding will be achieved only if plenty of live insects (tiny mealworms, fruit flies, and so on) can be supplied in addition to a good egg nestling food and insectivore mixture.

Most waxbills have sweet, high-pitched songs; some, such as the Strawberry Finches, are especially gifted in this respect.

Red-Billed Firefinch

The Red-Billed Firefinch or Senegal Firefinch (*Lagonosticta senegala*) comes from West Africa. The male is almost entirely pinkish-red in colour, fading to yellowish-brown underneath, and with brown wings and tail. The sides are spotted with tiny white spots. Bill, red; legs and feet, dark flesh colour. Length, 8.75cm (3.5in). The female is light brown, fading to whitish on the underparts.

This bird becomes tamer and more friendly than most waxbills and is quite hardy when acclimatised, although it does need heat during the winter months. It breeds freely, and the young are not too difficult to rear. The cocks fight during the breeding season so it is best to keep only one pair in an enclosure. They do not bother other birds.

The newly fledged young resemble the female in colour and show no red. Their bills are grey. Young cocks usually begin to show some red colouring when about six weeks of age.

Lavender Finch

The Lavender Finch (*Estrilda caerulescens*) comes from western and southern Africa. It is a delicate blue-grey, paler on the cheeks, and darkening toward the vent. A few white spots appear on the flanks and a black streak extends through the eye. The tail, rump, upper and under caudal feathers are deep crimson. Bill, black with lateral red streak. Legs and feet, black. Length, 10cm (4in). Sexes alike, although the feathers around the vent are usually somewhat lighter in colour on the female.

This species is somewhat delicate in captivity and is not often bred. The cocks are quite aggressive toward each other and fight savagely, so it is best to keep just one pair in a collection. They are also among the worst of the 'feather pluckers' and in crowded conditions end up miserable and ragged in appearance.

Cordonbleu Waxbill

One of the most beautiful of the waxbills is the Cordonbleu Waxbill (*Uraeginthus angolensis*) which ranges throughout tropical Africa in several races. The male's upper parts are brown; the face, breast and sides, bright blue. The abdomen and underparts are white-brown and the tail is dark blue. Its bill is red with flesh-coloured legs and feet. Length 11.25cm (4.5in). The female resembles the male but is slightly duller in colour.

This bird is quite hardy in captivity and a very free breeder, but not commonly imported. Dealers sometimes list it as the Blue-breasted Waxbill.

Red-Eared Cordonbleu Waxbill

The sub-species known as the Red-Eared Cordonbleu Waxbill (*Uraeginthus angolensis bengalus*), in which the male has bright red cheek patches, is the best known form of the species. It is slightly more delicate than the Cordonbleu Waxbill but, if kept fairly warm and fed properly (live insects and insectivore mixture in addition to seeds), it will live well and breed quite freely. Its nest should never be disturbed or looked into or the birds will desert it. Young birds resemble the female and cocks do not acquire the red cheek patches until about five months of age. Like the Firefinch this bird is quite steady and becomes fairly tame in captivity.

A red-headed Gouldian. This is one of the most colourful of all the finch species.

Red Eared Waxbill

The Red Eared Waxbill (*Estrilda troglodytes*) comes from West Africa and is the most commonly imported of all this group. It is greyish brown above, paler on the head. The underparts are greyish white with a pink patch on the abdomen. A streak of coral red extends from the base of the beak back through the eye. Tail, dark brown. Beak, red. Legs and feet, flesh-brown. The sexes are alike, although the female often shows less pink on the underparts. Length, 10cm (4in). This species is very difficult to breed in captivity, although some fanciers have had a measure of success. It is one of the waxbills that constructs a 'cock's nest' on top of the nest proper. Dealers often list the species as the Grey or Common Waxbill.

A Red-eared Cordonbleu Waxbill.

Orange-Cheeked Waxbill

The Orange-Cheeked Waxbill (*Estrilda melpoda*) is from western and eastern Africa. The head is light grey with bright orange cheeks; the back and wings, greyish brown; and the underparts, whitish. The rump is bright red and the tail is blackish brown. Bill, red; legs and feet, light brown. Length, 8.75cm (3.5in). The female is like the male but not quite so bright in colour and with smaller orange cheek patches.

This is a fairly hardy waxbill but nervous and a shy breeder. Young birds are similar to the adults except that the orange ear patches are smaller and paler in colour. The bill is black.

Strawberry Finch

Most popular of all the waxbills is perhaps the Strawberry Finch or Red Avadavat (*Amandava amandava*) which ranges from India through southern Asia and Malaysia. This is the only waxbill in which the male follows the example of the weavers and the whydahs and goes out of colour for part of the year. When it is in breeding plumage the upper parts of the head, back and wings are deep brown. The sides of the head, throat and underparts are scarlet. The flanks, wings and under tail coverts are spotted with white and the rump is bright red. Bill, red; legs and feet, pinkish. Length, 10cm (4in). The female is brown above, with darker wings, and yellow-buff below. Her rump and upper tail coverts are dark red, and she has a few white spots on the wings. The male resembles her when out of colour.

Strawberry and Lavender Finches.

This is the normal Gouldian Finch found in the wild in Australia.

Two forms of this bird are available. The larger, and more common one, is that described earlier which comes from India and is usually listed as the Bombay Avadavat or Tiger Finch. A smaller and usually more expensive form comes from Indo-China and Java and is known as the Chinese Avadavat. It is brighter red in colour and has a black abdomen.

This bird breeds readily, and the male is one of the waxbills with a real song. The plumage change is often a slow process and some individuals become quite dark, almost black, in colour after a few moults in captivity.

Gold-Breasted Waxbill

Smallest of all these birds is the Gold-Breasted Waxbill (*Amandava subflava*) from West Africa. It is olive-brown above with the throat, abdomen and under tail coverts golden yellow. The breast is bright orange, and a bright red streak passes over the eye. Bill, red; legs and feet flesh colour. Length, 7.5cm (3in). The female lacks the crimson eyebrow and her breast is not orange but pale yellow.

This tiny waxbill is quite hardy and breeds freely. It is one of the smallest of all finches and must be kept in cages or aviaries with very closely spaced bars. Some individuals seem to have a tendency to turn very dark in colour, sometimes almost black, after being in confinement for a while. Young birds are greyish brown in colour with darker wings. Their bills are black.

Silverbills are a very common type of finch.

GRASS FINCHES

The grassfinches are among the most popular of all finches in aviculture. They inhabit Australasia and Malaysia and are primarily found in Australia. Most of them are brightly coloured and many breed well in confinement. Many are unusual in that they drink by sucking up the water and swallowing without lifting their heads.

In the natural state, these finches frequent grasslands and brushland areas and live in small flocks. The courtship display is fairly simple. The cock sits still with his flank feathers puffed out, his neck stretched out in front of him, and his bill pointing downwards. During this time he sings a sort of melody with great effort, raising his body up and down with a twisting motion. In some species, the cock holds a blade of grass in his bill during the display. The nests are typical spherical structures, and the nestling birds show luminous mouth markings similar to those in the waxbills. The young are quite easy to rear since they feed mainly on seeds and green food which they eat themselves. Milk-soaked bread is a useful addition to the diet when young are in the nest. Some species will take insects.

All grassfinches are sociable and quite peaceful in mixed groups, although many will breed better kept in single pairs. Some of the hens are subject to egg-binding, and it is wiser to allow them to breed only in fairly warm weather; they should be well supplied with cuttlebone. Grassfinches usually appreciate nest boxes in which to sleep.

Diamond Sparrow
The Diamond Sparrow (*Steganopleura guttata*) comes from eastern Australia. Its upper parts are brownish grey; the forehead, head and nape are light grey; the rump and upper tail coverts, bright red; underparts, snowy-white; a black band extends across the breast and down each side where it is heavily spotted with white. Tail, black; bill, red; legs and feet, grey. Length, 12.5cm (5in). The sexes are alike in colouration.

This lovely bird is easy to keep but is very difficult to breed. The only way to determine the sex in these birds is by the male's song and courting dance. Young birds are mostly grey in colour with white breasts and underparts, and show the red rump from the first; their bills are dull grey. As well as the usual seed diet, Diamond Sparrows require a lot of insect food.

Star Finch
The Red-Tailed or Star Finch (*Poephila ruficauda*) comes from northern and eastern Australia. It is olive-green above, with the forehead, cheeks, and throat bright red, finely spotted white on the cheeks. The breast and sides are olive-grey, heavily spotted with white, and the centre of the abdomen is yellow. Tail, red; bill, red. The female is lighter in colour and shows less red on the face.

Left: The Australian Red-Tailed or Star Finch.

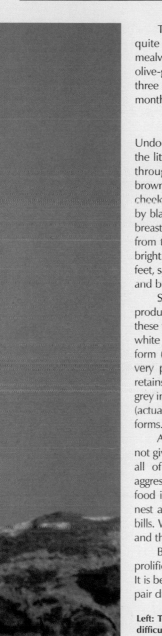

This species is hardy when acclimatised and breeds quite freely. The parents should be supplied with mealworms when rearing young. Immature birds are dull olive-green in colour and show no red until they are about three months of age. They come into full colour in about six months.

Zebra Finch

Undoubtedly the most common of all finches in captivity is the little Zebra Finch (*Poephila castanotis*), which is found throughout Australia. The upper parts are ash-grey, brownish on the wings. Tail is black with white bars. The cheeks are bright chestnut, with a white mark surrounded by black below and in front of the eye. Throat and upper breast are greyish white, barred with black, and separated from the white underparts by a heavy black band. Flanks, bright chestnut spotted with white; bill, orange; legs and feet, salmon. Length, 10cm (4in). The female is grey above and buff below and lacks all the bright markings.

Several colour variations of this bird have been produced in captivity and colour standards established for these forms. In addition to the normal (grey), there is a pure white which retains the orange-red bill and legs; a silver form (dilute normal) which retains all the markings but in very pale colour; and the fawn Zebra Finch which also retains the characteristic markings but is fawn rather than grey in colour. Pale forms of the latter are known as 'creams' (actually 'dilute forms'). There are also pied and 'marked' forms.

All these birds are easily bred in small nest boxes. Do not give too much nesting material, or the birds will spend all of their time building nests. The cocks are quite aggressive toward other birds when breeding. No special food is required for the young. The young birds leave the nest after about 16 days and are grey all over with black bills. When they are 10 to 12 weeks old, their bills turn red and the males start to acquire their coloured markings.

Being entirely domesticated, the Zebra Finch is very prolific and will breed the year around if allowed to do so. It is best to take no more than two or three clutches from a pair during the course of a year.

Left: The Diamond Sparrow is easy to keep but difficult to breed.

Long-Tailed Finch

Although not brightly coloured, the Long-Tailed Finch (*Poephila acuticauda*) is one of the most attractive of the grassfinches. It comes from northern and northwestern Australia. The upper parts are rosy brown, darker on the wings; the crown and sides

Long-Tailed Finch (*Poephila acuticauda*)

of the head are silvery grey. There is a large black bib on the throat, and the eyes are encircled by a black oval. Upper tail coverts and rump are white, with the latter crossed by a black band. Underparts, fawn; thighs, vent and underwing coverts, white. Tail, black, with the two central feathers elongated into two wires. Bill, yellow; legs and feet, red. Length, 15cm (6in). The sexes are alike.

Heck's Grassfinch

This is another form of the Long-Tailed grassfinch known as Heck's Grassfinch (*Poephila acuticauda hecki*), which has a bright red bill. Both forms are very free breeders in captivity, being among the most prolific of all the grassfinches, with the possible exception of the Zebra Finch. They can be quite quarrelsome when breeding, and pairs are best kept in an aviary by themselves. There are usually four or five white eggs in a clutch, and both birds incubate for a period of about 14 days. Young birds are more or less grey all over, paler underneath. Adult males usually have a somewhat larger bib on the throat than adult females.

Gouldian Finch

The most beautifully coloured grassfinch and, indeed, one of the most beautiful of all birds is the lovely Gouldian Finch (*Poephila gouldiae*) from Queensland and northern and northwestern Australia. The back and wings are grass-green; the forehead, crown and throat are red, surrounded by a line of black that in turn is followed by a wider line of bright turquoise blue that widens at the nape. The rump is light blue; the breast, deep purple; upper abdomen, orange; lower abdomen, yellow fading to white. Tail, black with the two central feathers longer than the others and pointed on the ends; bill, white with a red tip; legs and feet, pinkish. Length, 11.25cm (4.5in). The female is similar but duller in colour.

This bird is also seen (more commonly) with black on the head in place of the red, or (rarely) with orange-yellow in the same area. It is a somewhat difficult subject to keep in captivity in certain respects, sometimes dropping dead for no apparent reason at all. If good stock is obtained, however, it is not too difficult to breed. No insectivore or live food is required, and young are reared on seeds and green food exclusively.

Gouldians usually go to nest sometime around July. Since they are not very hardy with regard to temperature - and hens are subject to egg-binding - it is difficult to keep them in open outdoor aviaries in the colder climates.

Incubation lasts for approximately 16 days, and the hatchlings are greenish grey above and yellowish grey below; they do not show any of the colour pattern found on the adults. Adult plumage is not attained until six to twelve months of age. They are aggressive towards other birds.

Red-Faced Parrot Finch

Another very beautiful grassfinch is the Red-Faced Parrot Finch (*Erythrura psittacea*), which comes from New Caledonia. It is bright glossy green in colour, with the head, throat and upper breast, bright red. The rump and tail are also red. The bill is black; legs and feet, grey. Length, 11.25cm (4.5in). The sexes are alike although females sometimes show less red on the face.

This species is not common in captivity, but is quite easily kept and bred. In its native Pacific Island habitat it nests in holes in rocks and breeds in small colonies. The male builds the nest and helps with incubation, which extends for a period of about 14 days. The young leave the nest around 21 days after hatching, at which time they are dull green in colour and have a dull red tail. Some show a little red on the face but this varies with individuals. The lower mandible of the beak is bright yellow and gradually changes to black. Full adult colour is achieved by about four months. Parrot Finches do not do well in small cages.

Mannikins

The Mannikins or Nuns are the least colourful members of this family. They inhabit Africa, Asia, Malaysia and Australasia but are most numerous in the Malaysia and New Guinea regions.

Heck's Grassfinch.

Most of them live in large flocks which congregate near reed beds and grasslands. They have short, thick beaks and their food consists almost wholly of vegetable matter (seeds and greens), although some of the African forms eat a considerable number of insects.

The cocks perform a courtship dance resembling that of the grassfinches. Most of these birds are difficult to breed in captivity, although there are some that do so quite freely.

Nestlings show the luminous mouth markings characteristic of this family, but the pattern is unique to this group. The palate is marked with horseshoe-like dark lines or blotches and the gape has a swollen line, but shows no warts or lobes.

Some of these birds are quarrelsome and dangerous to smaller and weaker birds. Most are very hardy and live for many years in confinement.

Java Sparrow

A very popular finch, the Java Sparrow or Rice Bird (*Padda oryzivora*) came originally from Java and Bali but is also found throughout Malaysia. It is fairly large (13.75cm, 5.5in) and mainly a beautiful slate-grey in colour, with a black head and white cheeks. The abdomen is pinkish fading to white underneath, and the wing flights and tail feathers are black. The bill is very large and bright pink. Legs and feet, reddish. Sexes alike, but the female's beak is somewhat smaller at the base than the male's. A pure white form (with red bill and legs) has been produced in captivity.

The Java Sparrow makes an excellent cage or aviary bird but is inclined to bully smaller finches. It makes an excellent pet if taken from the nest and hand-reared. Its diet should contain 'paddy' or unhusked rice.

Imported wild-caught specimens are not easily bred, although the pure white form breeds readily. The period of incubation is about 14 days. Not all young birds in the nest of a white Java will necessarily be white; some may be grey and others may be partly white. The grey ones will never be anything but grey, but some of those showing whitish feathers may moult out all white, while others end up mottled and are known as calico Java Rice Birds.

The normal young Java is grey all over, darker on the head, and lacks the white cheek patches. Its beak is dark brown and the full adult plumage with a red beak is not assumed until about the age of five months. Java Sparrows are sometimes sold under the name 'Java Temple Birds'.

Cut-Throat Finch

The Cut-Throat or Ribbon Finch (*Amadina fasciata*) comes from Africa. The general colour is brown, darker on the wings, each feather edged with black and showing white spots on the sides of the abdomen. A bright red collar extends across the throat from ear to ear. Bill, yellowish white. The female is similar but lacks the crimson collar.

This species is somewhat inclined to bully smaller, weaker birds. It readily breeds in confinement in cage or aviary, and the eggs hatch in about 12 days. The young leave the nest after 21 days. Young males resemble their mother, not acquiring the crimson throat collar until the first moult.

Bronze Mannikin

The very tiny (7.5cm, 3in) Bronze Mannikin (*Lonchura cucullatus*) is found throughout tropical Africa. The crown, sides of the head and throat are black; the head is glossed with green. The upper parts, including wings, are grey-brown, with bronze-black spots on the shoulder. Rump and upper tail coverts possess irregular black and greyish markings. Tail, black; flanks and abdomen, white, streaked and barred with wavy black lines. The female is similar but slightly duller in colour.

This species will breed in captivity. The young birds are quite different in appearance from their parents. They show no black but are reddish brown all over with darker wings and tail.

Bengalese Finch

One of the most interesting of all the small mannikins is the Bengalese or Society Finch (*Lonchura domestica*). This is an entirely domestic form whose ancestry is not definitely known. It was produced over a period of many centuries by Chinese and Japanese breeders and comes in three colour varieties: pure white, chocolate and white, and fawn and white. As well as self (solid) colours, tri-coloured and crested forms are also sometimes seen. The dark markings are never found in exactly the same places on two different birds. The sexes are exactly alike in appearance, distinguishable only by the male's little song with which he constantly serenades his mate. This can be heard most clearly when the two birds are separated and out of each other's sight: the male's call is a single syllable note that the female answers with a three or four syllable call.

The Bengalese Finch is one of the most easily bred of all cage birds, breeding equally well in cage or aviary. It is often used as a foster parent for the young of other species of finch, as it will incubate and rear the young of birds considerably larger than itself; however, it will not feed any food other than seeds and greens, so it is not of much use in rearing birds such as waxbills.

Bengalese Finches should be given nest boxes for breeding and kept one pair to an enclosure because, although they do not quarrel, they all crowd in the same nest box to sleep, making it impossible for any one hen to incubate eggs. Young birds resemble their parents but have shorter tails.

Spice Finch

The Spice Finch or Nutmeg Mannikin (*Lonchura punctulata*) has a wide distribution throughout India, Ceylon, southern Asia and Malaysia. It is chocolate-brown above, darker on the head, with narrow light shaft streaks. Face and throat, deep chestnut. The abdomen is whitish buff; the breasts and sides, spotted white over brown. The tail is washed with yellow. Bill, bluish black; legs, grey. Length, 10cm (4in). The sexes are alike.

Millet, seen in the background, is a staple part of the Spice Finch's diet.

This species is not too difficult to breed if a true pair can be obtained. Spice Finches live well on seeds and greens alone, seldom touching insect food, although it should be offered to them. Bird dealers in India have been known to dye this bird different colours (usually green) and offer them as 'painted finches'!

Black-Headed Nun

The Black-Headed Nun or Chestnut Mannikin (*Lonchura ferruginosa*) ranges from the Himalayas through Indo-China. It is deep chestnut in colour with a black head, neck and abdomen. The bill is silvery grey. Length, 10cm (4in). The sexes are alike.

This bird seldom breeds in captivity but at one time was one of the most commonly imported of the so called nuns. Its toenails (like those of the related forms) seem to grow much too fast, and it is usually necessary to catch the birds regularly and trim their claws to prevent injuries and accidents. Of course, if you are inexperienced in this practice, you must seek assistance.

Young birds are pale brown all over; traces of black start to appear about four to five weeks after the young leave the nest.

Tri-Coloured Nun

The sub-species known as the Tri-Coloured Nun (*Lonchura malacca*) originated in India and Ceylon. It is chestnut-brown in colour, with the head and upper breast black. The lower breast and sides are pure white, and the middle of the abdomen and underparts are black. The bill is silver-grey. The sexes are alike.

This form has been bred in captivity on several occasions. They incubate for about 14 days, and the young leave the nest about 23 days later. All of these nuns like to sleep in nest boxes at night.

The weaverbirds (family Ploceidae) are a large group (156 species) of small seed-eating birds that resemble the typical finches in appearance. They are found mainly in Africa, but also inhabit Europe and Asia in some numbers. Their name comes from the elaborate and skillfully-woven nests that they construct.

WEAVERS AND WHYDAHS

Most of the species are quite hardy and may be kept in outdoor aviaries the year round once acclimatised. All of them may be fed on millet, canary and other small grass seeds with some soft food (insectivore mixture), as well as greens and fruit. They are also fond of mealworms. Make sure that grit, fresh water, and cuttlebone are always available.

The whydahs or widow birds are closely related to the weavers but are easily distinguished by their habit of scratching up the ground with their feet in the manner of game birds. Like the weaver cocks, whydah males go out of colour for part of the year.

They are parasitic nesters, and commonly deposit their eggs in the nests of certain waxbills. All are good aviary subjects and easily kept but are not easily bred in captivity because of their odd nesting habits. As with the typical weavers, they do not attain full adult plumage until their second year. The cocks are polygamous.

Orange Weaver
The most common and best known form is the Orange Weaver or Bishop (*Euplectes orix franciscana*)

Pin-tailed Whydah, (*Vidua macroura*)

of northeastern and western Africa. The male in breeding plumage is deep velvety black, with the neck, chin, breast, back and elongated tail coverts, orange-red. The wings are tawny with dark brown stripes. Bill and legs, greyish flesh coloured. Length, 6.25cm (2.5in). The older these birds are, the darker the orange-red becomes. When displaying, the feathers of the neck stand out and form a ruff. The female is light brown with dark streaks. As with most others of this group, it is very difficult to pick a pair when the male is out of colour. It is rarely bred in captivity.

Napoleon Weaver

The most common of the yellow and black weavers is the Napoleon or Golden-crowned Bishop (*Euplectes afra*) from western Africa. The male in colour is bright golden yellow with a velvety black face, chin, lower breast and abdomen. Wings and tail are brownish. Bill, black; legs, flesh coloured. Length 10cm (4in). The female is light brown, marked and streaked with darker brown, and her face and breast are somewhat yellowish. The male resembles her when out of colour.

This species has often bred in captivity, laying three or four white eggs, lightly speckled with brownish black; incubation lasts about 13 or 14 days.

Pin-Tailed Whydah

One of the most common of the long-tailed forms is the Pin-Tailed Whydah or Widow Bird (*Vidua macroura*) found throughout tropical Africa. When in colour the male is glossy black above; the underparts, sides of the head, lower back, and a stripe across the wings are white. The long (22.5cm, 9in) tail feathers are black and very narrow. Bill and legs red. Length (including tail), 32.5cm (13in). The female is tawny, speckled with black. This species is very quarrelsome.

Paradise Whydah

The best known and most popular whydah is the Paradise Whydah or Widow Bird (*Steganura paradisaea*) from Senegal and western Africa. The male when in colour is black with a very wide reddish brown collar around the neck and yellowish underparts. The two centre feathers of the tail are long (28.75cm, 11in) and plume-like; the two outer feathers shorter, wide at the base and narrowing to long, curled, wire-like ends. Beak, black; legs, flesh coloured. The female (and the male in eclipse) is reddish grey streaked with black. This is a very beautiful bird when in breeding plumage, is easily kept, and does not bother any other birds.

BIBLIOGRAPHY

**THE COMPLETE BOOK OF FINCHES
& SOFTBILLS**
David Alderton
ISBN 0-79380-511-2
TS-307

A comprehensive guide to all aspects of caring for and breeding these birds. Practical information on the different species, including specific housing and nutritional requirements.
Hardcover: 180mm x 260mm, 191 pages, colour photos throughout.

GUIDE TO OWNING A FINCH
Rod Fischer
ISBN 0-79382-010-3
RE-210

This exciting and beautifully photographed Finch book contains valuable and authoritative information. Anyone interested in purchasing one of these lovely birds, as well as those who already own one, will find this guide a must.
Softcover: 170mm x 250mm, 64 pages, colour photos throughout.

FINCHES
Curt Af Enehjelm
ISBN 0-86622-728-8
KW-027

This book presents easy-to-follow recommendations about selecting and caring for Australian Finches. It concentrates on providing readers with the information they need, all given in an interesting and easy to read style.
Hardcover: 145mm x 205mm, 128 pages, colour photos throughout.

PROPER CARE OF FINCHES
Phillip St Blazey
ISBN 0-79383-153-9
TW-100S

This book, written in an easy-to-read, interesting style, contains practical, sensible advice for the beginner about the do's and don'ts of keeping finches. An essential guide for anyone who owns finches.
Softcover: 130mm x 205mm, 256 pages, colour photos and drawings.

Useful Addresses

**Royal Society for the Prevention
of Cruelty to Animals
(RSPCA)**
Causeway, Horsham
West Sussex   RH12 1HG
Tel: 01403 264181

National Council for Aviculture
4 Haven Crescent
Werrington
Stoke-on-Trent
Staffs   ST9 0EY